Meaningful PRINT

Creating an Environment with Print-Rich Experiences

Written by Jeri A. Carroll

Illustrated by Janet Armbrust

Teaching & Learning Company

1204 Buchanan St., P.O. Box 10
Carthage, IL 62321-0010

This book belongs to

_____

Cover photo by Images and More Photography

Copyright © 1999, Teaching & Learning Company

ISBN No. 1-57310-192-3

Printing No. 987654321

Teaching & Learning Company
1204 Buchanan St., P.O. Box 10
Carthage, IL 62321-0010

Table of Contents

A special thanks to Debbie Mendoza, kindergarten teacher at Park Elementary in Wichita, Kansas, for translating the parent letters into Spanish.

Dear Teacher or Parent,

Why a book about providing meaningful print in early childhood classroom?

When should we teach children to read? Should we teach reading in preschool? Should we teach reading in kindergarten? Should we wait until tests of maturation tell us children are ready to read?

A joint position statement from the International Reading Association and the National Association for the Education of Young Children (*Young Children*, July 1998) tells us early exposure to meaningful reading and writing experiences is critical. "Failing to give children literacy experiences until they are school-age can severely limit the reading and writing levels they ultimately attain."

Our memories of learning to read often include small or large group reading experiences. The IRA/NAEYC position statement on learning to read and write suggests that young children need to have experiences that make reading and writing meaningful. Lessons and activities should build on prior learning rather than structured whole-group instruction or intensive drill and practice for groups or individuals. How can we provide those experiences?

In a print-rich environment, children can incorporate reading and writing into everyday experiences. They tell about meaningful life happenings, listen to meaningful stories, read about meaningful events and write about meaningful experiences. They incorporate reading, writing and storytelling into dramatic play. All of this exposes children to a variety of print and shows them the processes of reading for real purposes.

A balanced combination of playful experiences and meaningful instruction provides the best possible influence on children's literacy development.

Sincerely,

Jeri A. Carroll

TLC10192 Copyright © Teaching & Learning Company, Carthage, IL 62321-0010

ABOUT THIS BOOK

The purpose of this book is to show that if you

✏️ **provide** meaningful experiences in reading and writing

✏️ **demonstrate** the experiences

✏️ **model** their use

✏️ **choose** motivating learning activities in a print-rich environment

Then children will

✏️ **learn to enjoy** reading and writing

✏️ **feel confident** as they make their early attempts

✏️ **become successful and fluent** in these two essential areas

Provide a Print-Rich Environment

Check out the lists of reading and writing supplies on pages 8 to 10. How many of these do you have? How many could you get free or inexpensively? How many of these should go on a wish list to parents? "Children learn a lot about reading from the labels, signs and other kinds of print they see around them." (*Young Children*, 1998)

Do you have signs and posters in your room? Is there a calendar, a helper chart, an attendance chart, number words? See page 8 for other suggestions.

Check out the lists of materials on pages 11 to 13 that you may choose to provide in existing centers. How many do you have in the centers suggested? How many could you move to these centers rather easily? How many need to go on a wish list?

Do you have coupons (pages 40 to 45)? Can young children read these coupons or at least part of them?

Do you encourage children to collect menus, candy wrappers and cereal box panels that they can read? (See pages 46 to 51.)

How Many Do I Have?

Providing and Demonstrating

Using Print Meaningfully

Do you use print meaningfully in the classroom, or are children required to write letters and words because you require it?

Letter-Writing Experiences

Introduce letter-writing experiences, class autograph books, labeled photo albums, book making centers and personal and class journals (pages 46 to 55).

Language Experience Charts

Language experience charts are most beneficial at the pre and early reading stages. The teacher or parent writes as the children dictate their thoughts and experiences. This allows children to see the connection between the spoken word and the printed word (*Young Children*, 1988).

Sight Words

Post sight words (pages 63 to 65) and thematic or project vocabulary words in the classroom with picture clues or brief definitions as needed.

Alphabet Letters

Learning the letters of the alphabet allows children to see the connection between letters and sounds (*Young Children*, 1988). Do you encourage children to explore the alphabet not only with alphabet charts displayed in the room but in newspapers, books, catalogs, bulletin boards, menus, signs, billboards and posters? Use clues as they appear during the day, talking about it in an easy, natural manner—"Oh, here's a B again right on the bathroom door!"

Reading and Writing Experiences

Labeling Objects

Encourage children to label objects in pictures, their own possessions, items in the classroom and at home. Before long, children will begin to recognize words they have noticed in several different situations and locations.

Alphabet Books

Do you provide a variety of alphabet books in the classroom (see pages 86 to 91)? Read the books aloud several times using a consistent pattern (a is for apple, or big a, little a, apple) as you read the letters and pictures. A comprehensive bibliography and ways to use alphabet books are included.

Provide blank Alphabooks (pages 92 to 109) and other needed materials for teacher-made or child-made alphabet books. Demonstrate various ways to show how children might complete their books. You'll find new and interesting ideas in this book.

Do you ask parents if their children are interested in reading (page 113) and writing (page 122)? Do you observe children to see if they voluntarily choose to do reading and writing experiences? You'll find help in this book.

Do you save samples of children's writing experiences in an organized format (see information on portfolios on page 110)? Saving monthly writing samples is a marvelous way to show and compare the progress throughout the school year? It's an easy and ideal way to measure learning and growth for each child.

Environmental Checklists
Reading and Writing Supply Checklist

Having the following suggested materials on hand in your classroom will make your activities easy and quick to organize. Take inventory and check off your adequate supplies. Ask parents to donate others. Make a wish list for purchasing larger items with extra school funds.

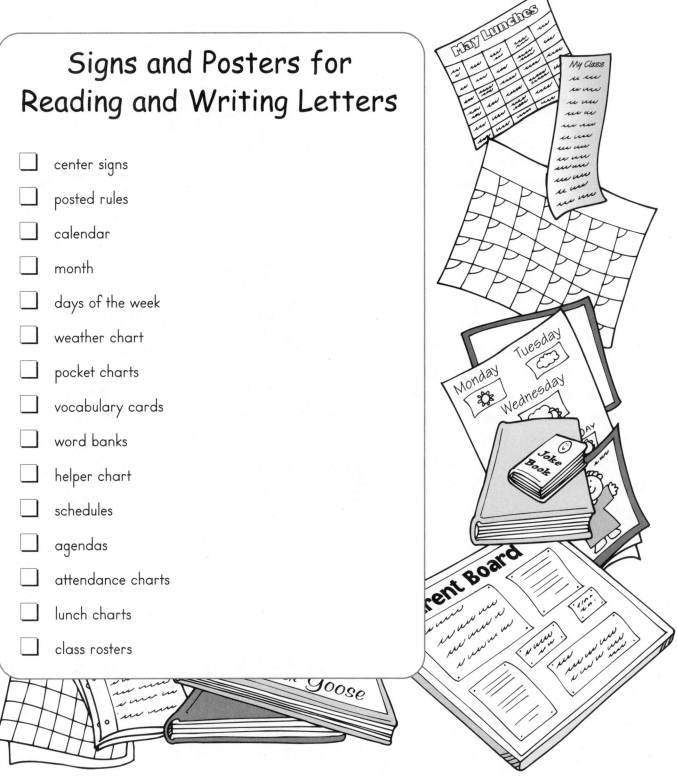

Signs and Posters for Reading and Writing Letters

- ☐ center signs
- ☐ posted rules
- ☐ calendar
- ☐ month
- ☐ days of the week
- ☐ weather chart
- ☐ pocket charts
- ☐ vocabulary cards
- ☐ word banks
- ☐ helper chart
- ☐ schedules
- ☐ agendas
- ☐ attendance charts
- ☐ lunch charts
- ☐ class rosters

Paper and Writing Utensils

- [ ] full sheets of paper in a variety of colors and weights
- [ ] picture story paper
- [ ] picture story paper on a roll
- [ ] ruled newsprint
- [ ] sentence strips
- [ ] lined chart paper
- [ ] unlined chart paper
- [ ] tablets
- [ ] spiral notebooks
- [ ] adding machine tape
- [ ] greeting cards
- [ ] envelopes
- [ ] mailbox
- [ ] fat pencils
- [ ] thin pencils
- [ ] colored pencils
- [ ] fine-tipped markers
- [ ] broad-tipped markers
- [ ] scented markers
- [ ] paint and paintbrushes
- [ ] standard crayons
- [ ] jumbo crayons
- [ ] painting crayons
- [ ] overhead projector

- [ ] overhead marking pens
- [ ] transparencies
- [ ] glue
- [ ] finger paint
- [ ] finger paint paper
- [ ] pudding to use as finger paint
- [ ] shaving cream to write letters in
- [ ] yarn for shaping letters
- [ ] small flower boxes for making letters in
- [ ] small sandboxes for making letters in
- [ ] salt boxes for making letters in
- [ ] sidewalk chalk
- [ ] chalkboards
- [ ] lined lap chalkboards
- [ ] unlined lap chalkboards
- [ ] chalkboard backings for shelving
- [ ] chalk
- [ ] colored chalk
- [ ] chalkboard erasers
- [ ] whiteboards

- [ ] unlined white lapboards
- [ ] lined white lapboards
- [ ] whiteboard backings for shelves
- [ ] whiteboard markers
- [ ] whiteboard rag
- [ ] magic slates
- [ ] check-in roster checklists in centers
- [ ] parent board
- [ ] story starters
- [ ] nursery rhymes
- [ ] poems
- [ ] jingles
- [ ] jokes

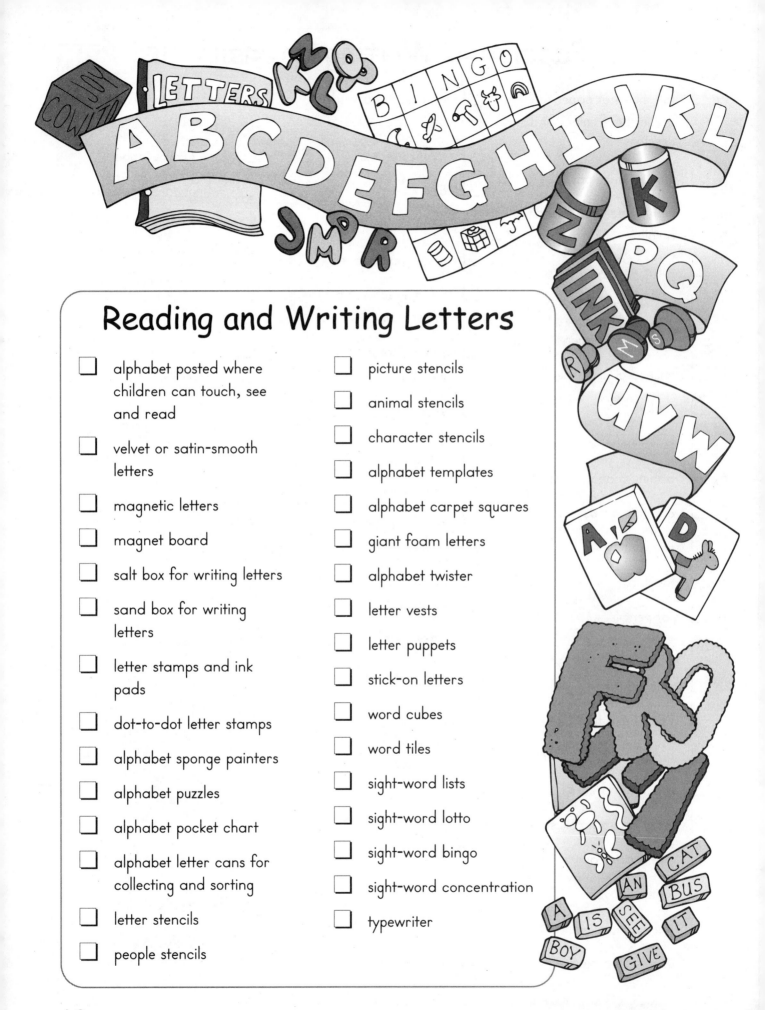

Reading and Writing Letters

- alphabet posted where children can touch, see and read
- velvet or satin-smooth letters
- magnetic letters
- magnet board
- salt box for writing letters
- sand box for writing letters
- letter stamps and ink pads
- dot-to-dot letter stamps
- alphabet sponge painters
- alphabet puzzles
- alphabet pocket chart
- alphabet letter cans for collecting and sorting
- letter stencils
- people stencils

- picture stencils
- animal stencils
- character stencils
- alphabet templates
- alphabet carpet squares
- giant foam letters
- alphabet twister
- letter vests
- letter puppets
- stick-on letters
- word cubes
- word tiles
- sight-word lists
- sight-word lotto
- sight-word bingo
- sight-word concentration
- typewriter

Storytelling Center

- [ ] hand puppets
- [ ] finger puppets
- [ ] theater
- [ ] felt board
- [ ] felt story characters
- [ ] storage pockets for pup-pets
- [ ] storytelling kits

Library Center

- [ ] easy access bookshelves
- [ ] storage cubes
- [ ] children's books
- [ ] Caldecott award books
- [ ] popular character children's books (Arthur, Barbie, Barney, Bat Man, Beauty and the Beast, Cinderella, Curious George, Little Bear, Little Mermaid, 101 Dalmatians, Peanuts, Peter Pan, Pocahontas, Sesame Street, Steve and Blue)
- [ ] children's picture dictionaries
- [ ] big book dictionaries
- [ ] children's encyclopedias
- [ ] picture and letter hardboard alphabet books
- [ ] picture and word alphabet books
- [ ] picture, word and sentence alphabet books
- [ ] picture, word and definition alphabet books

Reading and Writing Words, Sentences and Stories

- [ ] thematic or project word banks where children can touch, see and read
- [ ] thematic or project word lotto
- [ ] thematic or project vocabulary cards
- [ ] thematic or project word bingo
- [ ] thematic or project word concentration
- [ ] sing-along charts
- [ ] poetry charts
- [ ] fingerplay charts
- [ ] maps and map puzzles
- [ ] catalogs
- [ ] phone books

- [ ] newspapers
- [ ] magazines
- [ ] comics
- [ ] ads
- [ ] recipe books
- [ ] recipes
- [ ] graphs
- [ ] play money
- [ ] menus
- [ ] grocery lists
- [ ] traffic signs
- [ ] labels for supplies
- [ ] labels for equipment
- [ ] labels for manipulatives

Letter and Word Games

- [ ] Boggle®
- [ ] Boggle, Jr.®
- [ ] Scrabble®
- [ ] Scrabble, Jr.®

Providing a Print-Rich Environment

To encourage young children to read, provide many things for them to read. Make sure that plenty of motivating reading material is available in each area of the classroom.

Arts and Crafts Center

An arts and crafts table should have a variety of media, materials and supplies from which students can choose to make something creative. An arts and crafts table can also encourage reading and writing. Check your area to see if you have the following things:

- ☐ letter and number stamps
- ☐ letter and number stencils
- ☐ vocabulary cards (picture, word and brief definition)
- ☐ pencils and lined paper
- ☐ thank-you note card example (reproducible on page 14)

- ☐ invitation note card example (reproducible on page 14)
- ☐ birthday note card example (reproducible on page 15)
- ☐ note card example (reproducible on page 15)

Arts and Crafts

Card made and designed by

_____

Thank
You

- Cut here - - - - - -

Fold here

Card made and designed by

_____

You're
Invited

A Note
to You

Card made and designed by

_____

- - - - - - - - - - - - - - - - - - Cut here

Fold here

Happy
Birthday

Card made and designed by

_____

Most block play centers in early childhood classrooms contain a variety of blocks where children can construct objects and structures of their choice. You may want a sign for the center and add word labels to identify different types of blocks.

Block Center

Do you have these additional items in your block area to encourage reading and writing?

- [ ] picture and word labels for the blocks
- [ ] paper of various sizes and pencils
- [ ] crayons
- [ ] photo album of previously constructed structures with labels

- [ ] traffic signs
- [ ] billboards
- [ ] grid paper
- [ ] masking tape

Dramatic Play or Housekeeping Center

Materials and equipment to include in the dramatic play or housekeeping center include cupboards, a sink and stove, table and chairs, a doll bed, an ironing board and iron and perhaps a carpenter's bench. Dress-up clothes, a mirror, play jewelry and a variety of hats will give students the opportunity to role-play in a variety of situations. Provide labels to show where the items "live" so children can learn the words and know where they belong.

Stock this play area with the following print-rich supplies to accompany the hands-on items:

- ☐ *TV Guide*
- ☐ magazines
- ☐ daily newspaper
- ☐ books
- ☐ food boxes
- ☐ food cartons
- ☐ food cans with labels

- ☐ phone book
- ☐ sacks and bags from various stores
- ☐ grocery list note pad (reproducible on page 41)
- ☐ personal phone and address book (reproducible on page 18)

Class Phonebook Entry

_____
name

_____
address

_____
phone number

Class Phonebook Entry

_____
name

_____
address

_____
phone number

Class Phonebook Entry

_____
name

_____
address

_____
phone number

Class Phonebook Entry

_____
name

_____
address

_____
phone number

18

Reading Center

Most early childhood classrooms set aside a comfortable and cozy place where children can go to read on their own. Examine yours! Do you have inviting items that are commonly found in a reading corner?

Do you have these items?

- ☐ an inviting and colorful area with a beanbag chair or small couch
- ☐ comfortable pillows
- ☐ simple picture-word books
- ☐ books you have already read to the students
- ☐ book posters mounted on the wall or folding screen
- ☐ books to accompany your thematic unit or current project

- ☐ advertising sections from daily news-papers
- ☐ magazines
- ☐ comics
- ☐ ads
- ☐ coupons
- ☐ class photo albums (labeled)
- ☐ phone books
- ☐ catalogs (early childhood equipment and clothing)

Writing Center

An early childhood writing center should have a variety of writing materials including pencils, chalk, fine- and broad-tipped markers and crayons plus a variety of paper in assorted sizes—some lined, some unlined. Check to see that your center includes these items. Add the following for a motivating and fun place that children will want to spend time at:

- [ ] picture dictionaries
- [ ] whiteboard and markers
- [ ] chalkboards and erasers
- [ ] stencils
- [ ] laminated letters, words and patterns for tracing
- [ ] alphabet templates
- [ ] simple to complex, dot-to-dot laminated sheets
- [ ] English vocabulary cards (related to unit or project)
- [ ] Spanish vocabulary cards (related to unit or project)

Children's Books

Brown, Marc. *Arthur Writes a Story*. Little, Brown, 1996.

Moss, Marissa. *Amelia's Notebook*. Tricycle Press, 1995.

Moss, Marissa. *Amelia Writes Again*. Tricycle Press, 1996.

Rumford, James. *The Cloudmakers*. Houghton Mifflin, 1996.

Stevens, Janet. *From Pictures to Words*. Holiday House, 1995.

Teague, Mark. *How I Spent My Summer Vacation*. Crown, 1995.

Turner, Priscilla. *The War Between the Vowels and the Consonants*. Farrar, Straus & Giroux, Inc., 1996.

20

Math Center

Your math center may be filled with manipulatives, numbers, counters, containers, puzzles, pocket charts, pegboards, tangrams, parquetry blocks, magnetic boards, clocks, dice, beads and even a calculator. There are many reading and writing activities related to numbers that can spark new learning.

Check your math center for these items:

☐ paper of various sizes, shapes and colors

☐ pencils of various sizes and colors

☐ number and counting books

☐ number, word, object charts

☐ written problem-solving strips

☐ calendar pocket chart with months and days of the week

☐ number word cards

☐ phone books

☐ grocery ads showing prices in large print

☐ catalogs

☐ beginning number bingo game

Science Center

Early childhood science centers are usually stocked with ant farms, butterfly gardens, ladybug farms, magnifying glasses, color paddles, live animals, plants, sense stimulators, simple machines, tops and perhaps a microscope.

Check your science center for reading and writing items:

- ☐ variety of shapes, sizes and colors of paper
- ☐ variety of colors and sizes of markers and pencils
- ☐ whiteboard and markers
- ☐ chalkboard and chalk
- ☐ individual science recording journals
- ☐ class recording journal

- ☐ labels for each item
- ☐ life science books
- ☐ science alphabet books
- ☐ science counting books
- ☐ life cycle charts
- ☐ recording sheets for experiments
- ☐ stencils
- ☐ weather chart and information

Charts and Signs

So much goes on in an early childhood room! Be sure to label each of these items to encourage your children to read (and perhaps write) and also inform others about what is going on.

Make or use charts and signs for each of the following in English and Spanish if needed:

April

Cloudy

Arts and Crafts

Coats, Hats, Boots

August

Cots

Backpacks

Computers

Blocks

December

Circle Time

Dramatic Play

February

Housekeeping

Foggy

January

Games

June

Geography

July

Grocery

Library

Gross Motor

Listening Center

Health

Lunch Boxes

Manipulatives	November
Maps	Numbers 1-10 10 1 3 4 6 8 2 5 7 9
March	Numbers 11-20 11 12 14 16 20 18 13 15 17 19
Math Center	Numbers 21-30 21 23 25 27 28 22 24 26 29 30
May	October
Music	Parent Board ATTENTION PARENTS
Nap Zone (Sleeping Children)	Pitch, Bounce and Toss

Puzzles

Stormy

Rainy

Sunny

Reading Center

Water Table

Sand Table

Windy

Science

Woodworking

September

BACK TO SCHOOL

Writing

Snowy

Zoo

CHILDREN'S BOOKS

The number of appealing and attractive children's books has increased enormously in the past few years. Books come in a variety of sizes and shapes, in various formats and in a never-ending assortment of subjects. Visit your local children's bookstore and neighborhood library frequently to see the latest new titles that may be suitable for your classroom. Ask your local bookseller for free promotional book posters they are no longer using. Decorate your reading center with these colorful wall hangings to provide an appealing place to be.

Just putting good children's books in your room, however, does not necessarily mean that the children will go to them, look at them, try to read them or ask to have them read. How do you motivate children to do that? There are several things to keep in mind.

✎ Be sure that you have a wide variety of books available for children.

✎ Change hardback books with frequent trips to the library.

✎ Purchase reference books that are on the level of your children.

✎ Provide parents and children with book club order forms.

✎ Provide children with books that portray both sexes in varying roles.

✎ Provide books portraying multicultural illustrations.

✎ Select Caldecott and Newbery award winners.

✎ Find out the favorite children's authors and start collections of these books.

✎ Provide a wide selection of books on the topics of your current, past and future themes and projects.

✎ Provide both purchased and library books in your room to show children the various ways to acquire books to read.

CHILDREN'S BOOKS

Reading Levels

Provide children with books at a variety of reading levels. In order to insure a variety of reading levels, examine the books for the number, repetition and difficulty of the words in them.

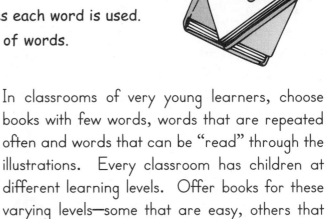

- Write down the title of the book.
- Make a list of each word in the book.
- Tally the number of times each word is used.
- Record the total number of words.

In classrooms of very young learners, choose books with few words, words that are repeated often and words that can be "read" through the illustrations. Every classroom has children at different learning levels. Offer books for these varying levels—some that are easy, others that challenge at a slightly higher level.

Don't worry about offering books that children may be exposed to next year. Familiar books become favorites and rereading them when children have advanced skills will make them feel successful.

28

CHILDREN'S BOOKS

Placement of Various Types of Books

ABC Board Books

Many people choose simple ABC board books only for infants and toddlers. However, they make excellent, and durable, beginning reading materials for young children. Have some available in the dramatic play center in your room where your youngest learners will tend to play. Some children may even be able to read them to others!

Picture Dictionaries

Very young children use picture dictionaries much like they use the simple picture-word ABC board books—to find pictures they know and label them with words. Eventually they will make the connection between the picture and the word—perhaps with a little help. Place these in a dramatic play center or at a writing table where students can draw pictures and write the words on cards.

Children's Science Books

Many different books serve as science books. Some ABC books are on specific science topics such as gardens, vegetables, frogs, bugs and fish. Place several in the science center or "let's find out" center. Select those that are project or theme related, and change them regularly to keep children interested and curious about new books.

CHILDREN'S BOOKS

Motivation

Model

As with most other learning that takes place in early childhood classrooms, model your reading habits for your students. Show your desire and general love of books. Show children books you are reading, explain your enjoyment of rereading a favorite book and teach students to respect and care for books. Refer to a variety of books for information as the need occurs.

Books in Good Condition

When children use books without being taught how to care for and respect them, books are frequently torn, written in, misused and generally made unappealing for other students. Teach the proper care of books. Show children how to turn pages properly by gently turning the top right corner of the page. Discourage children from turning a page by moving it brusquely with their hand as this easily and permanently wrinkles the pages. Teach the proper care of books.

Storing Books

Make sure the books have a good storage area and are within children's reach. When shelves are not available, turn an empty box on its side and use as a shelf. Cover it with wallpaper; gift wrap or clear, self-adhesive paper and use it as a shelf.

Store books standing with the bindings showing for ease of selection. However, remember that young children cannot yet read the bindings and will need to see the front covers to make choices. Display as many books as you can standing open for children to see the covers and inside pages.

Read and Reread

Reading aloud to children and allowing them to be active participants in the reading helps to build skills essential for reading success. Children "talk about the pictures, retell the story, discuss their favorite actions and request multiple rereadings" (*Young Children*, 1998). In some cases the rereadings allow children to bring in more of their personal experiences to connect with the author's messages.

CHILDREN'S BOOKS

Read and Display

If you want young children to read, expose them to books that have been read to them. When you read and reread a book to children, place it where they can pick it up and "read" it for themselves. When books have simple pictures, one predictable word per page or frequently repeated words, children will begin to "read" the books from memory.

Do not discourage children from reading books from memory.

Big Books

Big books also help children learn about print and how it carries the meaning of the story. Use big books to demonstrate how reading progresses from left to right and from top to bottom. See if children can match words from a page in a big book to other words in class. "In the course of reading stories, teachers may demonstrate these features by pointing to individual words, directing children's attention to where to begin reading and helping children to recognize letter shapes and sounds." (*Young Children*, 1998).

Reading with Props

When you read or tell children their favorite stories, use a variety of puppets to make the story come alive. Inexpensive puppets can be made from paper bags, socks or gloves. Flannel board cut-outs also provide graphic excitement to a story. Leave props out after using them. Encourage children to use them as they read to a classmate and improvise and act out favorite parts and scenes.

Provide a space where children can read to one another, to stuffed animals and to dolls. Make the use of the book and props easily accessible. When children first start, they will probably only use the props and retell a story. Retelling of stories leads to a child's emerging ability to read independently.

USING PRINT MEANINGFULLY

Young children will model what others around them do. As most of us know, that means the good things and the bad things. Think about everything you might do in a classroom each day. How much of the time do you spend writing? What is it that you are writing? Do you keep writing materials close at hand in several areas of the room? Do you have note pads, permission slips and report forms out where students can see them?

After you give your room a "print check" using information in the section called Print-Rich Environment, provide an opportunity for children to participate in the following activities.

Letter Writing

Fill the writing center with writing pads and envelopes. Ask parents for addresses of friends and relatives that children might write to. (See page 34 for a parent letter or page 35 for a Spanish translation.)

Young children can draw a picture, send a copy of something they have done in school or dictate a letter to someone older who can write it for them.

Provide a sample letter format for those children who are at the writing stage. (See page 36.)

USING PRINT MEANINGFULLY

Class Mailbox

Purchase or construct a mailbox to place on a counter in your room. Have children submit designs for painting it. Select one or a combination of a few.

Paint the outline of the design onto the mailbox using a thick black line. Let each child in the class paint a portion.

Secret Writing Pals

When children do not have interest in writing and mailing letters to people far away and do not get quick responses, allow them to have secret writing pals in the room. Assign each child a child in the room. Encourage the child to draw a picture or write a note, put it in the envelope or just fold it over and staple it. Children put the letters in a class mailbox during the day.

At the last recess, check to see that there is a message for everyone in the mailbox. For those who do not, provide a little memo (a note to tell them they look nice today, a note about their new shoes, a note about how good their lunch looked).

At the end of the day, let children receive notes from their secret writing pals.

Pen Pals or E-Mail Pals

Older children may be ready for pen pals or e-mail pals. Many of you know teachers who have moved to different schools, cities, states or countries. Contact them about the possibility of setting up pen pals or e-mail pals. If you don't, cooperate with another class in a neighboring school as pen pals or e-mail pals.

Children's Resources

Ahlberg, Janet., and Ahlberg, Allan. *The Jolly Postman.* Great Britain: Wm. Heinemann Ltd., 1986.

Keats, Ezra Jack. *A Letter to Amy.* New York: Harper, 1968.

Keats, Ezra Jack. *A Letter to Amy* on *The Ezra Jack Keats Library* (video). Weston, CT: Children's Circle, 1993.

Dear Families,

Children are preparing to write letters for the first time to family members and friends. We have a special area in the room for letter writing with paper, pencils, erasers, envelopes and crayons and stickers for decorating letters. I have displayed some envelopes and letters recently received to provide a personal touch.

Let your child see you address an envelope and write a letter at home. It would be helpful if you would send friends' or relatives' names and complete addresses so that your child may write and mail letters to the persons you designate.

Once the letters are finished, children will put them in envelopes and address them. I will send the letters home for you to stamp and mail with your child. Children will be eager to receive responses!

Thanks for your help!

_____

Teacher

_____
Full name of person you will write

_____
Street address

_____
City, State, Zip

Dear _____ ;
        the name you call the person

_____
Full name of person you will write

_____
Street address

_____
City, State, Zip

Dear _____ ;
        the name you call the person

_____
Full name of person you will write

_____
Street address

_____
City, State, Zip

Dear _____ ;
        the name you call the person

_____
Full name of person you will write

_____
Street address

_____
City, State, Zip

Dear _____ ;
        the name you call the person

Estimadas Families,

Los niños preparan para escribir cartas a sus familiares y amigos. Tenemos un lugar especial en el salón donde se encuentra papel y lápices, goma y sobres, crayones y calcomanías para decorar las cartas. He mostrado unos sobres y cartas como ejemplos para que los estudiantes los vean.

Deje que su niño lo vea dirigiendo un sobre y escribiendo una carta en casa. Sería útil si mandaría los nombres y direcciones de amigos o familiares de su niño que usted gustaría que escribieran.

Al terminar las cartas, los niños las pondrán en los sobres y a los sobres les pondrán las direcciones. Yo enviaré las cartas a casa para que ustedes les pongan el sello y con su niño las manden por correo. Los niños esperarían anisosamente una respuesta.

¡Gracias por su ayuda!

_____

Maestro

_____
Nombre completo de persona

_____
Dirección

_____
Ciudád, Estado, Zona Postal

Querido/a _____ ;

_____
Nombre completo de persona

_____
Dirección

_____
Ciudád, Estado, Zona Postal

Querido/a _____ ;

_____
Nombre completo de persona

_____
Dirección

_____
Ciudád, Estado, Zona Postal

Querido/a _____ ;

_____
Nombre completo de persona

_____
Dirección

_____
Ciudád, Estado, Zona Postal

Querido/a _____ ;

Date _____

_____
Full name of person you will write

_____
Street address

_____
City, State, Zip

Dear _____,
    the name of the person you are writing

_____
_____
_____
_____
_____
_____
_____
_____
_____
_____

Sincerely,

_____
Your name

USING PRINT MEANINGFULLY

Autograph Books

Purchase or make a small autograph book. Cut out the face portion from each child's school photograph and glue one photo to each page.

Place the autograph book in the reading center. Move it to the writing center periodically so children can write on their page (front and back) at various times of the year.

If you make a book each year, you will have a method of remembering all your children.

Jeff
I like cats.

My name is Molly.

OUR FIELD TRIPS

Mrs. Cusey's Farm

Puppies, Puppies, Puppies!

John is feeding a goat.

Baby chickens are chicks.
Tina

I held a baby piglet.

Class Photo Album

Take photos of children or groups of children, making sure to include every child in each roll of film.

Once the film is developed, place the pictures on the writing table or near the computer for children to examine. Encourage them to write or dictate one-line statements about the pictures and leave them with the picture. Mount the photos and student captions onto paper and display on a low bulletin board or photo album for easy reading.

USING PRINT MEANINGFULLY

Book-Making Center

Provide book-making materials at a center where children can assemble their own books to write whenever they choose.

Have on hand
- writing paper of various sizes, shapes and colors (use with adult supervision)
- staplers (use with adult supervision)
- three-hole punches (use with adult supervision)
- three-ring folders
- card stock for book covers

Hardboard Book Covers

To make a hardboard book cover for a set of stapled pages, you will need two pieces of hardboard (backs of tablets, cardboard, backs of cereal boxes, poster board or matte board). Cut the pieces of hardboard the same width as the cut paper, but slightly larger in height than the pages of the desired book.

Lay a strip of 2" (5 cm) wide mailing tape 1" (2.5 cm) longer than two times the length of your book on the table, sticky-side up. Place one cover 1/2" (1.25 cm) onto the tape, 1" (2.5 cm) from the bottom. Place the other cover on the opposite side of the tape.

Bring the long piece of tape down over the top of the covers and tape. Bring the short piece of tape up. Fold the two pieces of cardboard over so a book cover is made.

Once the entire cover is made, place the stapled book pages where children have written or will write their stories so that the stapled part is centered in the tape. Staple the cover and pages together through the tape.

38

USING PRINT MEANINGFULLY

Teacher-Made Books

Make several blank books of various sizes and shapes. Keep them easily available. Use them to record experience stories from important events, special holidays, field trips or parties. Read them to the children frequently, and put them in the reading center for children to read independently or to one another.

Class Journal

Purchase a blank book at the beginning of the year. At the end of the day, each day, work with the children to see what they would like you to record for that day in school. Rewrite what they say into words and/or pictures that they can "read."

For the very young, draw pictures of what they did using stick figures. Label with one-word or two-word captions.

For beginning readers, provide pictures with a one-line simple sentence.

For slightly advanced readers, provide a picture and a simple story about what you did during the day.

Have the journal available for children to read—in the reading corner, the class library or on your desk.

USING PRINT MEANINGFULLY

Coupon Reading

Many young children are very familiar with newspapers, grocery ads and coupons. Children can learn to read from these types of print—in the classroom and at home. They may have learned to recognize the names of favorite and familiar products on the store shelves at an early age. Children can then transfer this learning and recognize these products in pictures and in logos. Supply your room with the following items and copies of the grocery lists on page 41.

Newspapers

Grocery Ads

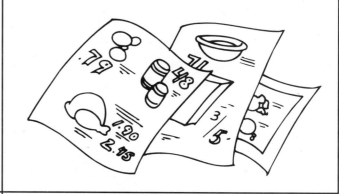

Current Booklets

Expired Coupons

Empty Product Containers

Advertising Supplements

Shopping List

_____

_____

_____

_____

_____

_____

_____

_____

Don't Forget!

_____

_____

_____

_____

_____

_____

_____

Grocery List

_____

_____

_____

_____

_____

_____

At the Store

_____

_____

_____

_____

_____

_____

_____

Using Coupons in the Classroom

Dear Families,

During the next few weeks we will be using coupons in the classroom for a variety of activities. Please send us your expired coupons, unused coupons from the Sunday inserts of the newspaper and grocery ads.

We will be cutting out coupons, sorting them by food groups, making grocery lists, shopping, designing our own lists and creating fun activities as the students explore coupons.

If you would like your child to cut out the coupons and return them for your use, please send an envelope with your name on it along with the coupons.

Keep your eyes open for coupons for the next few weeks!

Thanks!

_____

Teacher

Usando Cupones en el Salón

Estimadas Familias,

Durante las próximas semanas, usaremos cupones en el salón para algunas actividades. Por favor mandenos cupones no usadas que se encuentran en el periódico del domingo y también los anuncios de las tiendas.

Vamos a cortar y separar los cupones en grupos de comidas, haciendo listas de compras, haciendo compras y otras actividades divertidas mientras los niños exploran los cupones.

Si quiere que su niño le devuelva los cupones, mande un sobre con su nombre y los cupones.

Estén en busca por cupones en estas semanas.

¡Gracias!

_____

Maestro

COUPONS

In addition to teaching children scissor skills involving arts and crafts projects, try having students follow the dashed lines on coupons for a different and meaningful skill activity.

Place coupon sheets or books in a center with scissors, a small box for clipped coupons and a larger box for paper scraps. Have children cut out coupons for classroom use, or if they bring their own sheets from home, have them cut them out for their families.

Coupon Pocket Charts

Make a pocket chart using a different color for each food group. Place the title of the food group at the top and cut out pictures from grocery ads to show what the food group is.

About 5" (13 cm) below the title, place 1" (2.5 cm) strips of white poster board across the chart. Place the glue at the bottom of the strip only, leaving the top of the strip loose from the chart. Continue placing these strips down the chart about every 5" to 6" (13 to 15 cm).

As children cut out their coupons, they may place the coupons in the "pockets" of these charts.

COUPONS

Reinforced Coupons

Gather coupons from the newspapers, coupon books and from parents. Glue the coupons onto coupon-shaped pieces of poster board. Laminate and cut out.

Sort Coupons

Make coupon-sorting containers from the bottoms of milk cartons. Cut the milk carton off about halfway up. Put a word and picture on the carton to indicate what types of coupons should be put into the carton. Let children sort the coupons into the containers, and then place them in a standard coupon sorter.

Matching Product to Coupon

As you cut out the coupon from the coupon booklets, many times there are also pictures of the products close by. Cut out the picture of the product and glue it on a separate piece of poster board using different colors to keep them visually separate from the coupons. Laminate and cut out.

Toss all the coupons and product pictures into a large container, and let children separate the coupons and product pictures. Then match the products to the coupons.

COUPONS

Going Shopping

Make sure that you have both a housekeeping dramatic play area and a grocery store center in the classroom. Place coupons and newspaper ads in the housekeeping area to match the products in the grocery store center. Put blank grocery lists, pencils, play money, wallets and purses in the housekeeping area. Add a cash register, grocery aprons and shopping bags in the grocery store center.

Let the children make grocery lists in the housekeeping area, take a grocery cart to their "grocery store" area and select and purchase the groceries they need. Return them to their "home" and cook up a couple of good meals.

Designing Coupons

Provide children with coupon-sized pieces of paper, and have them draw or cut out pictures of the products they wish to have coupons for. Older children may write the name of the product and a price for the coupon. Glue them onto pieces of poster board. Laminate them for use in the centers.

What Do We Need?

Plan a meal for the children to make in the classroom. Examine the recipes for the ingredients. (Read *Pancakes for Breakfast* by Tomie de Paola.) Write the name of each ingredient on a separate card. Sort the cards into types of foods or into sections in the grocery store. Put the ingredients on a grocery list. Check the class coupons for usable coupons.

Take a walking trip to a local grocery and purchase the ingredients, checking each off as it is placed in the basket. Ask for a subtotal before coupons and a total after coupons. Back in the room, using real money, show the children how much they saved. Talk about what they can do with money saved.

SCRAPBOOKS, NOTEBOOKS AND PHOTO ALBUMS

Collecting written information and placing it in scrapbooks, notebooks and/or photo albums provides meaningful reading for children, especially if they are doing the collecting themselves—independently or as a class.

On the next few pages you will find suggested topics, methods of collecting reading material and suggested title pages for your books. Use the title pages in the sizes provided, or enlarge to fit the first full page of your book.

Scrapbook Reading

Provide newspapers, magazines, scissors, scrapbooks and a topic the children are interested in or are studying (Ex: Foods). Have them go on a hunt to find foods in the grocery ads that show the food and the written word, either on the can or package and/or written near it. Children cut out the food item and the corresponding word and glue them onto a page of the scrapbook. A clever title will help motivate the collection and the reading.

Let's Go Shopping

Collect logos from store sacks and shopping bags.

Following are some suggested titles for scrapbook reading.

What's for Snack?

Bring snack food labels from home.

I'm Thirsty

Search for soda and juice ads.

What's for Breakfast?

Bring front panels of cereal boxes from home.

What's the Cost?

Collect pictures and prices from newspaper ads.

SCRAPBOOKS, NOTEBOOKS AND PHOTO ALBUMS

Notebook Reading

Place several acetate sheet protectors in a three-ring, loose-leaf binder. Encourage children to collect and place "meaningful print" that has information on two sides. The sheet protector allows students to read both sides of all collected information.

Provide children with scissors, sheet protectors, magazines, catalogs, coupon inserts and writing materials to begin their collection.

Following are some suggested title pages for notebook reading.

Let's Eat Out

Collect menus from restaurants.

Who's Playing Baseball?

Collect sports trading cards.

What's for Breakfast?

Use the fronts and backs of cereal boxes.

Yum! Yum! Candy

Place candy wrappers in protector sheets.

Keep on Chewing

Collect gum wrappers and/or gum packages.

SCRAPBOOKS, NOTEBOOKS AND PHOTO ALBUMS

Photo Album Reading

Photo albums with "magnetic" protector sheets allow another way to collect reading information for children. A class field trip captured in photographs would allow children the chance to tell the story of the field trip in pictures and words. Young children can be encouraged to give one-word captions for the pictures. Older children could give simple sentences.

Following are some suggested title pages for photo album reading.

In the Movies

Collect movie titles from news ads.

Cut out pictures from movie reviews.

Car Shopping

Collect names of cars from newspaper and magazine ads.

Paste the car picture near the name.

Shoes in the News

Collect shoe pictures from ads.

Label each shoe type or brand.

Toys

Collect pictures of toys from toy ads.

Place label on or near toy.

Months of the Year

Use photos from old calendars with the months labeled.

54

SCRAPBOOKS, NOTEBOOKS AND PHOTO ALBUMS

Here are some additional suggested theme-related, picture-reading activities.

Use any format (scrapbook, notebook or photo album) to collect meaningful reading on these topics as well.

Favorite Stories

Let child draw a title page from a favorite story.

Write story name below picture.

Our Feathered Friends

Collect pictures of birds.

Label each picture.

On the Farm

Take or collect photos children bring from home.

Label each item.

A Rainbow of Vegetables

Collect photographs of vegetables.

Sort by color. Label with color word and vegetable name.

Singing Songs

Draw a picture depicting a song.

Write the title at the top.

Write the words on the page.

Whose Bears Are These?

Take photos of each child's teddy bear.

Write each child's name under the bear.

SIGHT WORDS

Some words in our language are used with greater frequency than others. *Sight words* are those words which children are taught to recognize strictly on sight. These words don't use phonics or other decoding methods for recognition. Sight words have been compiled into lists—Fry Instant Words, Ekwall Basic Sight Words and the Dolch Word List.

Sights words such as *the, when* and *have* are successfully taught using word cards and age-appropriate lists of sight words appear with great frequency in beginning readers. Children learn to recognize these words through a variety of reading experiences. In keeping with developmentally appropriate practice, these words should be taught using activities that are real and relevant.

Frequent exposure to the sight words on class charts, signs and posters as well as in books and class activities will allow students to readily become familiar with the words. Appropriate sight words should be connected to themes and subjects children are learning about.

A Rainbow of Sight Words

Post sight word lists on long strips of paper. Divide the words into groups of five or 10 words, depending on your students' level. Write the words on colored sheets of paper, displaying them in order: red, orange, yellow, green, blue. Use light shades of each color and a broad black marker to make words easy to read. If using colored poster board, list a second group of words on the reverse.

Post the words in the classroom. As you come across them in big books, point them out to the children and show the words on charts. As you write experience stories with children, point the words out. As children approach the charts, read the words to them and have them point to and repeat them after you.

Sight Word Fishing

Sight Word Fishing Cards

Make a set of sight words based on your students' levels. Use a blank deck of playing cards or unlined index cards. Make a second set identical to the first. To easily sort the different levels into proper packs, use round colored labels or stickers and affix to the back of each card. Level 1—red sticker. Level 2—orange sticker. Level 3—yellow sticker. Level 4—green sticker. Level 5—blue. For additional levels, use two red stickers, etc.

Pond

Cut out a large pond shape from a piece of blue construction or butcher paper.

Game

Play Sight Word Fishing with a group of two to four students. Mix both groups of cards from one level together. Deal four cards to each child. Have students hold the cards in their hands. Put all of the other cards face side down on the pond.

Have each child check his or her cards to look for any matches. All matches should be placed on the table (or floor) in front of the player who has them.

One child begins and checks his or her cards to see the words. That player may then ask the others if they have a matching card. If a child has one, it must be given to the player who asked for it. The player then places both matching cards in front of him. The player gets a chance to ask again.

If the child asked doesn't have the match, he or she says, "Go fish." The player who has asked for the card then goes to the extra cards in the pond and picks one. If it matches, the match is placed in front of the child, and he or she continues to ask for cards. If it doesn't match, the card is kept in the hand, and the play continues to the player on the left.

Play ends when all cards are gone from the pond and all matches have been made.

Sight Word Concentration

Sight Word Concentration Cards

Use the same set of sight word cards as used for Sight Word Fishing.

Game

The first player turns one card over, faceup, in the same position it was placed. Player selects a second card and again turns it faceup in the same place. Player observes the two words to see if they are the same. (Older students may read the words; younger children may look for similarities or word configurations.)

If the words are the same, the player picks them up and places them in front. Repeat by turning over two more cards. If they are not the same, the cards are turned back, facedown in the same place and the game moves to the player on the left.

If the cards are the same, the player picks them up, places them in front and turns over another set of cards. If they are not the same, the cards are turned back over in their exact spot and play moves to the next player to the left.

Play continues until all cards are matched.

Sight Word Bingo

Sight Word Bingo Cards

Make four copies of blank 5" x 5" (13 x 13 cm) bingo cards (page 60) on card stock. The center square is free. Using colored construction paper, cut up small squares to be used as markers.

Select two consecutive levels of sight words totaling about 20 words. Write the words in random order in the blanks on the bingo cards. Words may be used more than once.

Sight Word Cards for the "Caller"

Using the same words on the bingo cards, make a set of calling cards with one word on each card for the caller. (If the teacher or an adult is the caller, words may be called directly from a list.)

Game

The game may be played with two to five students.

Select one child to be the "caller." The caller has the stack of mixed-up sight word cards.

All other players have a blank bingo card and markers. The caller picks up one of the sight word cards and holds it up for the others to see. The players look to see if they have the sight word on their bingo card. If they do, they place a marker on it. If they do not, they wait for the next word to be called.

Young children may only look for the matches visually. Older children may say the word when they hold up the card. Advanced children may call the word and not show it to the players as they search for the match.

When a player gets all words in a row covered either horizontally, vertically or diagonally, he calls "bingo." Player must call out words to the caller who checks that the words have been called.

As a variation, game may also be played where students must cover the entire card instead of only one row.

BINGO

		FREE		

Sight Word Lotto

Sight Word Lotto Board

For each level of sight words, run two copies of the Sight Word Lotto Board on page 62. Use heavyweight paper or card stock. Print one set of sight words on each of the lotto boards in the same order.

Mount one of the Sight Word Lotto Boards onto a piece of matte board. Color-code the levels by using different colors.

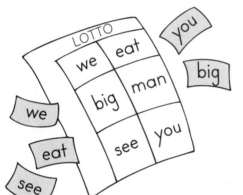

Sight Word Lotto Cards

Cut the other board into individual word squares.

Game

Individually children may take the cards and match them to the word on the board, placing the card over the word on the board.

If two children are playing together, one child has the cards and the other has the board and blank markers.

The child with the cards holds up one card at a time and shows it to the player

with the board. (If they can read the words, have them read the word to the player.) The player finds the matching word on the board and places a marker on the board. Play continues until all words are covered.

Lotto Board

LOTTO

Sight Words

(From Ekwall Basic Sight Words, Fry Instant Words and Dolch Sight Words)

Preprimer	here	said	ate
a	I	see	be
and	in	the	black
away	is	three	brown
big	it	to	but
blue	jump	two	came
can	little	up	did
cannot	look	we	do
come	make	where	eat
down	me	you	four
find	my		get
fun	not	**Primer**	good
funny	one	all	have
go	play	are	he
help	run	at	into

like	that	**First Grade**	him
must	there		his
new	they	after	how
no	this	an	just
now	too	any	know
on	under	as	let
our	want	ask	live
out	was	by	may
please	well	could	of
pretty	went	every	off
ran	what	fly	once
ride	white	from	open
saw	who	give	over
say	will	going	put
she	with	had	round
so	yes	has	some
soon		her	stop

take	buy	many	why
thank	call	pull	wish
them	cold	read	work
think	does	right	would
walk	doing	sing	write
were	give	sit	your
when	fast	sleep	
	first	tell	
Second	five	their	
Grade	found	these	
always	gave	those	
around	goes	upon	
because	green	us	
been	hot	use	
before	its	very	
best	let's	wash	
both	made	which	

VOCABULARY

Teachers need to capitalize on every opportunity to enhance children's vocabulary development, through the reading of stories, explanation of vocabulary words before reading and meaningful use in and out of the classroom. (*Young Children*, 1998)

As new words appear associated with themes, projects or stories, incorporate them into the visual world of the students. Place the written words and pictures to indicate definitions in a word bank, on segments of a word worm, in a class dictionary or on vocabulary word cards.

Word Bank

As themes or projects progress, unfamiliar words will appear.

Make a large cut-outs from poster board of the shape of the concepts being examined (apple, car, star, horse). Laminate the cut-out shapes before writing the new vocabulary words on them.

As the words appear, record the words on the cut-out shapes. Younger children will need picture clues. Use simple black-line drawings, or cut out pictures and affix to the cut-outs with sticky tack. More advanced children may need only the word. Independent readers may need a short definition.

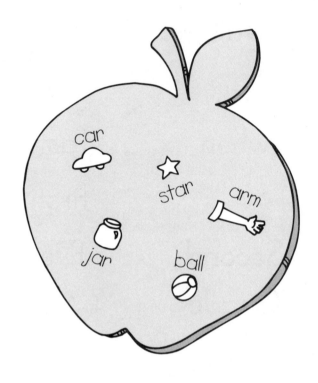

Class Dictionary

Provide a three-ring binder to serve as a class dictionary. As each new word appears in themes, projects or stories, write the word on a sheet of paper and illustrate (pictures, photos or drawings). Pages may then be rearranged in alphabetical order.

Separate books may be made for each project, theme or story.

VOCABULARY

Word Worm

Use the head below to begin a word worm in your classroom. Copy it onto green paper. Decorate with ribbon, glitter, wiggly eyes, etc.

Cut out a cardboard pattern the same size as the circle used for the worm's head. Each time a new vocabulary word is introduced, assign a child to trace and cut a new segment for the worm. Write the word on the segment and select a student to illustrate it—or use a photo from a magazine or catalog. If your students no longer need picture clues, you may print the words on the segments without illustrations.

VOCABULARY

Vocabulary Fishing

Vocabulary Fishing Cards

Print two identical sets of vocabulary words on a deck of blank playing cards or index cards. Place a sticker on the back of the card to note the theme or project (apples, shoes, grocery, fire fighter). For older children, make one set with the word and one with the picture.

Pond

Make a blue felt or paper pond.

Game

Use the rules for Sight Word Fishing (page 57).

Vocabulary Concentration

Vocabulary Fishing Cards

Print a set of thematic vocabulary words on a set of blank playing cards or index cards. Make a second set identical to the first, or for older children have one set with words and one set with pictures. Keep track of the themes by stickers on the backs of the cards.

Game

See the rules for Sight Word Concentration (page 58).

Vocabulary Bingo

Vocabulary Bingo Cards

Make four copies of blank 5" x 5" (13 x 13 cm) bingo cards (page 60) on card stock. The center square of the card is free.

Write vocabulary words in random order on the cards, using the words more than once.

Vocabulary Word Cards for the "Caller"

Make a set of cards using the same vocabulary words or the pictures.

Game

Play the game using the same guidelines given for Sight Word Bingo (page 59).

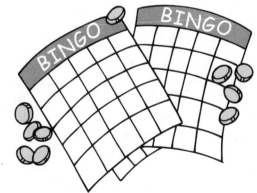

68

VOCABULARY

Vocabulary Word Lotto

For each set of vocabulary words, run two copies of the Lotto Board (page 62) on card stock. Print one set of vocabulary words on one board, and draw or paste a picture of the word on the other.

Vocabulary Word Lotto Board

Mount one of the Vocabulary Lotto Boards on a piece of matte board.

Vocabulary Lotto Cards

Cut the other board into separate word pieces.

Game

Use the rules for Sight Word Lotto (page 61).

Vocabulary Word Cards

For each theme project, make a class set of vocabulary cards. Cards may have the word on one side and the picture on the other, or the word and picture on the same side. Punch a hole in the upper left-hand corner of the cards and put them on a binder ring.

Alphabetizing the Vocabulary

Make an alphabet pocket chart from 26 library pockets and a piece of poster board, or make one with cloth pockets.

Have children place the vocabulary cards in the pockets according to the first letter of the word.

If removed in order, children can write the words in alphabetical order.

Personal Vocabulary Cards

Provide materials for the children to make their own vocabulary cards.

Include class vocabulary cards, paper, markers, catalogs, magazines, pictures, glue, binder rings, envelopes, library pockets.

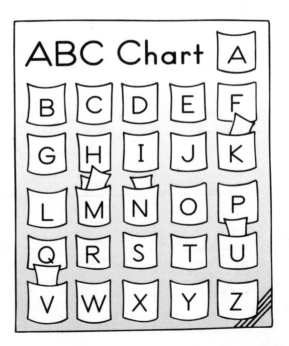

Exploring Letters

Alphabet Letter and Picture Cards

Aa		Bb	
Cc		Dd	
Ee		Ff	
Gg		Hh	
Ii		Jj	
Kk		Ll	

Mm		Nn	
Oo		Pp	
Qq		Rr	
Ss		Tt	
Uu		Vv	
Ww		Xx	
Yy		Zz	

Spanish Vocabulary Cards

Aa árbol tree	**Bb** bebé baby	**Cc** casa house	**Ch ch** chifle whistle
Dd diez ten	**Ee** elefante elephant	**Ff** foca seal	**Gg** gato cat
Hh hoja leaf	**Ii** imán magnet	**Jj** jabón soap	**Kk** kayac kayak
Ll luna moon	**Ll ll** llave key	**Mn** mano hand	**Nn** nube cloud

Spanish Vocabulary Cards

Ññ ñandú ostrich	**Oo** oso bear	**Pp** pluma pen	**Qq** queso cheese
Rr reloj watch	**Rr rr** correo mail	**Ss** sol sun	**Tt** tiza chalk
Uu uva grape	**Vv** vaca cow	**Ww** wagón wagon	**Xx** xilófono xylophone
Yy yate yacht	**Zz** zorra fox		

Learning Letters Allows Children to See the Connection Between Letters and Sounds

apple

Alphabet Boards

Make an alphabet board with 26 letter pockets. Use the letter-picture cards on pages 70 and 71 to place on library pockets. Make vocabulary cards for each class unit or theme. Write a word at one end of a 3" x 5" (8 x 13 cm) card, and place an illustration upside down at the opposite end so that the word or illustration shows when the cards are in the pockets.

When children have difficulty alphabetizing, let them make word cards, place them in the chart, pull them out in order and write them.

EXPLORING LETTERS

Letter Stickies

Cut out the letter-picture cards on pages 70 and 71 and enlarge. Paste each at the top of a half sheet of poster board. Post in the classroom for children to glue on pictures, letters, words and small objects that start with the letter.

Bulletin Board Alphabet Train

Cut out each of the alphabet letter-picture cards (pages 70 and 71). Enlarge them for bulletin board use. Cut the letters apart from the pictures, and glue both parts on a 3" x 5" (8 x 13 cm) card. Then glue wheels to each card, making a train boxcar. Design an engine from black paper. Make an alphabet train for use in the classroom.

Countertop Alphabet Boxcars

Glue each of the pictures onto small boxes. Place them on a countertop in the classroom and have children place small items in each that start with the corresponding letter.

EXPLORING LETTERS

Using Letter Pages

Letter pages can become essential learning tools in your classroom. Children can easily construct their own work with minimal teacher guidance. Listed below—in sequential order of difficulty—are a variety of ways these pages can be used. Assign pages to children according to their individual levels.

Letter Page Activities

Potato Stamp

Use a knife to cut individual letters to make potato stamps. Apply thick tempera paint to the letter and stamp on a page several times. Send the page home as "wrapping paper." Children should return with a small object that begins with the same letter wrapped in the paper. Place items on unfolded paper with letters showing and display.

Letter Stamps

Use letter stamps to match the letter, and stamp the letter onto the page.

Shaving Cream

Laminate paper. Spread shaving cream on the paper. Have children practice writing the letters in the shaving cream with their fingers.

EXPLORING LETTERS

Pasta Letters

Use dry pasta and glue to form letters in the center of the page and glue to the paper.

Unit Blocks

Provide the children with unit blocks and let them construct the letter in the center of the paper.

Many Times, Many Colors

Write the letter several times on the page using a variety of media: pencils, colored pencils, crayons, watercolors, markers, colored glue, etc.

Alphabet Macaroni Book

As a class, make an alphabet macaroni book. Place the letter sheets around the room. Provide alphabet macaroni and glue. As children find a letter, have them locate the correct sheet and glue on the macaroni.

Have the children write a large letter in the center of the paper and create something from the letter.

Big Letters from Small Letters

Form a large letter using several smaller letters.

EXPLORING LETTERS

Letter Rainbow

Make a rainbow using the letter. Form a letter arch of each of these colors: red, orange, yellow, green, blue, purple.

Letter Cut-Outs

Cut out letters from magazines, catalogs or newspapers and glue them onto the page.

Tactile Letters

Write one upper- and one lowercase letter. Glue on a tactile item that begins with the corresponding letter (wire for W, LifeSavers® for L, etc.).

Sparkly or Sandy Letters

Write a large letter in the center of the page. Cover it with glue. Sprinkle glitter or sand on the letter.

Letter Town

Draw a large capital letter with gray watercolors. Create a town using the gray letter as the roads. Give your town a name that starts with the letter.

Letter Patterns

Practice writing the uppercase and lowercase letters to form a pattern of . . .

78

EXPLORING LETTERS

Words

Locate words that start with the letter in newspapers, magazines, catalogs, etc. Cut out and glue onto the letter page.

Breakfast ABCs

Locate the names of breakfast items in newspapers, coupons or on boxes. Cut out and glue onto the correct letter pages to make a breakfast book.

At the Store

Locate the names of stores in newspapers and advertising inserts. Cut out and glue onto the correct letter page.

Beginning Sound Pictures

Locate pictures that start with the letter sound. Cut out and glue onto the letter page.

Friends

Find a friend in the room, in your family, in your school or in a story whose name begins with the letter. Perhaps it will be one of the teachers. Write the friend's name and draw a picture on the letter page.

EXPLORING LETTERS

Scavenger Hunt

Give each child a piece of paper with a different letter and a small paper sack. Find and collect items indoors or out that start with the letter. Return to the room. Place the items on the paper, and have the children phonetically sound out the word to write on the paper.

Sight Words

Provide children with sight word charts. Have them locate the sight words that begin with a specific letter and write them on their letter page.

Sounds and Sizes

Have children make a list of 10 things that start with the letter and are smaller than their desks, larger than their shoes and about the same size as their cars.

In the Movies

Use the movie ads from the newspaper. Cut out movie titles which begin with a specific letter, and glue titles onto the page.

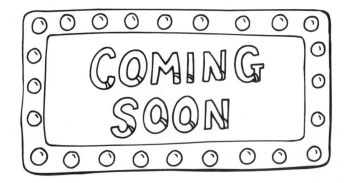

COMING SOON

TLC10192 Copyright © Teaching & Learning Company, Carthage, IL 62321-0010

EXPLORING LETTERS

Videos

Locate videos in the ads of the Sunday supplements. Cut out and glue onto the page that shows which letter the title starts with.

In the Library

Use books in the classroom and library. Record the titles of favorite books on the correct page, matching the first letter of the title with the letter page.

In the Word

Have children look around the room and find items that have their specific letter sound in them. Write the words that have the letter sound in them.

Beginning Dictionary Page

Give each child a set of pages. Have students collect words that begin with each letter from their reading, from picture dictionaries, from home, etc.

Letter Poem

After children have brainstormed or collected words which begin with a certain letter, have them create a letter poem using words that begin with that letter.

EXPLORING LETTERS

Short Vowels in the Middle

Have children draw pictures of words that have a specific short vowel sound in the middle. Phonetically sound out and write the words.

Handwriting

Children practice writing the letter several times in cursive. Have them circle their best.

Long Vowels in the Middle

Have children draw pictures of words that have a specific long vowel sound in the middle. Phonetically sound out and write the words.

Word Pages

Provide each child with a set of pages. By using their picture dictionaries, students can fill each page with words and pictures to "read" in their spare time.

82

EXPLORING LETTERS

Dictionary Pages

Provide each child with a set of pages. Have students create personal dictionaries by writing words on the pages whose definitions they do not know. Use dictionaries to locate definitions. Write or draw the definitions.

Sentences

After children have collected many words that begin with a certain letter, have them write sentences that contain only words that start with a certain letter. Illustrate the sentences and post them in the room. Let the class read their sentences to younger children.

Stories

Using pages from their individual dictionaries, have children write stories using a specific letter. Illustrate and bind. Read the stories to younger students in the school.

ALPHABET BOOKS AS READING BOOKS

Some of the first books that children commonly have read to them are alphabet and picture board books. Usually these beginning books contain only a picture, a picture and a beginning letter or a picture and one word. As children become familiar with these books, it is natural for them to try to read and name the letters and words independently.

The selection of alphabet books for early learners is appealing and attractive with a varied range in sizes, prices and bindings. Some are meant exclusively for the very youngest learners, others are for beginning readers and some are designed to be read to a child by an adult. Refer to the extensive lists on pages 86 to 88 to see which alphabet books are suitable for your students. Select those that are appropriate for current classroom units and themes.

Types of Alphabet Books

How can you determine which titles to use for your children? Examine your books and examine the types of print in each book. Categorize these books by the types and levels of print. Use these indicators and see how many the book has. These indicators are in sequential order of ease for a child to read.

Letters and pictures

Letters, pictures and words

Letters, pictures and simple sentences

Letters, pictures and definitions

This last type of book is closer to a simple dictionary rather than a simple alphabet book.

ALPHABET BOOKS AS READING BOOKS

Alphabet Letter and Picture Books

The simplest books of this type have the letter of the alphabet on a page with a photograph that starts with the letter.

More advanced books of this type have a letter of the alphabet on a page and pictures of several things on the page that start with the letter.

Some of these books will have only the uppercase letter. Some will have only the lowercase letter. Some will have both.

Alphabet Letter, Picture and Word Books

The simplest books of this type have a letter of the alphabet, a picture of a familiar object that starts with that letter and the word.

More advanced books of this type have the letter of the alphabet, pictures of several familiar objects that start with the letter and a word labeling each picture.

Alphabet Letter, Picture and Sentence Books

These alphabet books have not only the letter, picture and word but also have a simple sentence defining the picture or illustrating the word in a sentence.

Alphabet Letter, Picture and Definition Books

Picture dictionaries fit into this category and many different types should be available for children's use.

Individual subjects such as books on animals, insects, flowers, vegetables and transportation contain the letter and word but may also contain factual information. These books are appealing to young learners who have a particular interest in a subject. They are meant to be read to children who may then want to look through the book by themselves. After reading them to children, keep them available in a reading corner or class library for children to read on their own.

ALPHABET BOOKS AS READING BOOKS

Alphabet Letter and Picture Books

Hirashima, Jean. *ABC*. New York: Random House, 1994.

Scarry, Richard. *Cars and Trucks from A to Z*. New York: Random House, 1990.

Shevett, Anita, and Steve Shevett. *Baby's ABC*. New York: Random House, 1986.

Alphabet Letter, Picture and Word Books

Base, Graene. *Animalia*. New York: Harry N. Abrams, 1987.

Baynton, Sandra. *A to Z*. New York: Simon & Schuster, 1995.

Bender, Robert. *A to Z Beastly Jamboree*. New York: Lodestar Books, 1996.

Bond, Michael. *Paddington's ABC*. New York: Penguin Books, 1991.

Disney. *Disney ABC Babies*. Racine, WI: Western Publishing Company, 1996.

Ehlert, Lois. *Eating the Alphabet*. San Diego, CA: Harcourt Brace Jovanovich, 1989.

Geddes, Anne. *ABC*. San Rafael, CA: Cedco Publishing Company, 1995.

Hofbauer, Michele Pace. *All the Letters*. Bridgeport, CT: Greene Bark Press, 1993.

Hoban, Tana. *26 Letters and 99 Cents*. New York, Scholastic, 1987.

MacDonald, Suse. *Alphabatics*. New York: Trumpet, 1986.

Milne, Alan Alexander. *Winnie the Pooh's ABC*. New York: Penguin, 1995.

Murphy, Chuck. *My First Book of the Alphabet*. New York: Scholastic, 1993.

Patrick, Denise Lewis. Illustrated by Kate Gleeson. *Animal ABCs*. Racine, WI: Western Publishing Company, 1990.

Peterson, Roger Tory. *ABC of Birds*. New York: Universe Publishing, 1995.

Schories, Pat. *Over Under in the Garden*. New York: Farrar, Straus & Giroux, Inc., 1996.

Tapahonso, Lucy. Illustrated by Eleanor Schick. *Navajo ABC: A Dine Alphabet Book*. New York: Simon & Schuster, 1995.

Wood, Jerri. *Animal Parade*. New York: Scholastic, 1993.

ALPHABET BOOKS AS READING BOOKS

Alphabet Letter, Picture and Sentence Books

Adams, Pam. *Mr. Lion's I Spy.* Wilts, England: Child's Play, 1984.

Archambault, John, and Bill Martin Jr. *Chicka Chicka Boom Boom.* New York: Scholastic, 1991. (no letter/picture association but a catchy text)

Baker, Alan. *Black and White Rabbits ABC.* New York: Scholastic, 1994.

Bayer, Jane. *A My Name Is Alice.* New York: Trumpet Club, 1984.

Carter, David. *Alpha Bugs.* New York: Scholastic, 1994.

Downey, Jill. *Alphabet Puzzle.* New York: Lothrop, Lee and Shepherd Books, 1988.

Drucker, Malka. Illustrated by Rita Pocock. *A Jewish Holiday ABC.* New York: Trumpet, 1996.

Edwards, Michelle. *Alef-Bet: A Hebrew Alphabet Book.* New York: Lothrop, Lee and Shepard Books, 1992. (also contains the Hebrew alphabet)

Elting, Mary, and M. Folsom. *Q Is for Duck.* New York: Scholastic, 1980.

Ferguson, Don. *Winnie the Pooh's A to Zzzzzzz.* New York: Disney Press, 1992.

Greenfield, Eloise. *Aaron and Gayla's Alphabet Book.* New York: Black Butterfly Children's Books, 1994.

Hague, Kathleen. *Alphabears: An ABC Book.* New York: Henry Holt and Co., 1991.

Johnson, Audean. *A to Z Look and See.* Toronto, Ontario: Random House Ltd., 1989.

Jordan, Martin, and Tanis Jordan. *Amazon Alphabet.* New York: Kingfisher, 1996.

Kunin, Claudia. *My Hanukkah Alphabet.* Racine, WI: Western Publishing Company, 1993.

Lionni, Leo. *The Alphabet Tree.* New York: Trumpet Club, 1990.

Matthiesen, Thomas. *ABC: An Alphabet Book.* New York: Platt and Munk, 1982.

Mayer, Mercer. *Little Monsters Alphabet Book.* Racine, WI: Western Publishing Co., 1979.

Moore, Yvette, and Jo Bannatyne-Cugnet. *A Prairie Alphabet.* Montreal, Quebec: Tundra, 1994.

Peyo. *The Smurf ABC Book.* New York: Random House, 1983.

Potter, Beatrix. *Peter Rabbit's ABC.* London, England: Penguin Group, 1987.

Reasoner, Charles, and Vicky Hardt. *Alphabites.* Price Stern Sloan, Inc., 1989.

Sardegna, Jill. *K Is for Kiss Good Night.* A Bedtime Alphabet. New York: Bantam Doubleday Dell Publishing, 1996.

Seeley, Laura. *The Book of Shadow Boxes.* Atlanta, GA: Peachtree Publishers, Ltd., 1990.

Seuss, Dr. *Dr. Seuss's ABC.* New York: Random House, 1996.

ALPHABET BOOKS AS READING BOOKS

Alphabet Letter, Picture and Definition Books

Dodson, Peter. *An Alphabet of Dinosaurs.* New York: Syron Press Visual Pub., 1995.

Fain, Kathleen. *Handsigns.* New York: Scholastic, 1993. (also includes the hand sign)

Miller, Jane. *Farm Alphabet Book.* New York: Scholastic, 1987.

Pallotta, Jerry. *The Dinosaur Alphabet Book.* Watertown, MA: Charlesbridge Pub., 1990.

Pallotta, Jerry. *The Flower Alphabet Book.* Watertown, MA: Charlesbridge Pub., 1990.

Pallotta, Jerry. *The Freshwater Alphabet Book.* Watertown, MA: Charlesbridge Pub., 1996.

Pallotta, Jerry. *The Frog Alphabet Book.* Watertown, MA: Charlesbridge Pub., 1990.

Pallotta, Jerry. *The Icky Bug Alphabet Book.* Watertown, MA: Charlesbridge Pub., 1990.

Pallotta, Jerry. *The Ocean Alphabet Book.* Watertown, MA: Charlesbridge Pub., 1990.

Pallotta, Jerry. *The Underwater Alphabet Book.* Watertown, MA: Charlesbridge Pub., 1991.

Pallotta, Jerry. *The Victory Garden Vegetable Alphabet Book.* Watertown, MA: Charlesbridge Pub., 1992.

Pallotta, Jerry. *The Yucky Reptile Alphabet Book.* Watertown, MA: Charlesbridge Pub., 1990.

Ryden, Hope. *The ABC of Crawlers and Flyers.* New York: Clarion, 1996.

ALPHABET BOOKS AS READING BOOKS

Making Alphabet Books with and for Children

Letter and Picture

After reading books that show letters and pictures, make personal books for children.

Alphabet Picture Book

Purchase a blank book. Save the front page for a title page. Put a letter on each left-hand page. Help children find pictures to cut out. Glue them on the corresponding right-hand pages.

Complete the book by using letter blends (bl, br, cl, er, etc.) or digraphs (sh, wh, th, ch) and eventually numbers, depending on the size of the book.

Alphabet Photo Album

As children begin to show interest in letters, provide them with familiar pictures to associate with the letters.

Collect photos of familiar people and places and put them in an alphabetical photo album. As you read the book with children, start the page with *J is for Jeri* and let a child name the other people. Avoid forcing the statement, "J is for . . ." as children will automatically begin to use the phrase.

Letter, Picture and Word

As children start to show interest in words, read alphabet books that have pictures and words. Simply add words to the above books or start a new one.

Three-Ring Folder Books

Place 28 pages in a three-ring pocket folder. Save page one for a title page. Print a letter in the upper left-hand corner of each page, encouraging the child to look to that corner to start reading.

Place pictures on the pages that show the beginning letter. Print the word or have the children print the word below the picture.

ALPHABET BOOKS AS READING BOOKS

Letter, Picture and Sentence

When children read alphabet books that have letters, pictures and words, they will eventually start to tell you about the picture, usually something simple like "I love to eat apples." "I have a soccer ball." Capture these sentences and add them to your existing alphabet word and picture books or start a new one.

Sometimes a fourth or fifth grade class will take on the project of making an alphabet book for a younger class. Encourage them to make one of your school, city or state.

Spiral Notebook

Skipping the first page to use as a title page, write an alphabet letter on each succeeding right-hand page in the upper left-hand corner.

Find or draw small pictures that start with each letter on the appropriate page. As you read the book, record what the child says and write a sentence about the item.

Letters, Pictures and Definitions

As an introduction to dictionaries, allow children to make their own alphabet books with letters, pictures and simple definitions.

Favorite Things Alphabet Book

Provide 9" x 12" (23 x 30 cm) sheets of writing paper, unlined at the top and lined at the bottom. Encourage each child to draw a picture of a favorite object at the top of the page, write the word on the first set of lines and write a simple sentence below. Collect them over time. When the children are ready, have them put the pictures in alphabetical order and bind them.

90

ALPHABET BOOKS AS READING BOOKS

Alphabet Tapes, CDs, Videos and Other Resources

Children's Television Workshop. *ABC DEF GHI on Sesame Street Platinum: All Time Favorites* (CD). New York: Sony Wonder, 1995.

Children's Television Workshop. *Learning About Letters* (video). New York: Sony Wonder, 1986.

Children's Television Workshop. *Sesame Street Sing, Hoot and Howl* (video). New York: Sony Wonder, 1991.

Children's Television Workshop. *Sesame Street: The Bird Is the Word: Big Bird's Favorite Songs* (CD). New York: Sony Wonder, 1995.

Lyons Group. *Alphabet Soup on Barney Songs* (video). Allen, TX: The Lyons Group, 1995.

Palmer, Hap. "Bean Bag Alphabet Rag" on *Follow Along Songs* (video). Racine, WI: Western Publishing Company, 1992.

Pearson, Debora. *Alphabake! A Cookbook and Cookie Cutter Set.* New York: Dutton's Childrens Books, 1995.

Scarry, Richard. *Richard Scarry's Best ABC Video Ever!* (video). New York: Random House, 1989.

Seuss, Dr. *Dr. Seuss's ABC* (read-along book and audiotape) (video). New York: Random House Video, 1989.

ALPHABOOKS

After children have spent time "reading" alphabet board books with only letters and pictures, demonstrate how they might make their own. Use homemade blank books, spiral-bound notebooks, blank sheets of paper to be glue-bound or comb bound, or magnetic sheet photo albums. To make a class board book, use matte board and rings.

Making Blank Alphabooks

Fold seven sheets of paper in half. Staple three times near the center fold. Have children start with letter A on the front sheet and write each letter of the alphabet on each succeeding sheet, using both the front and back of the paper.

Provide younger children who might need picture clues with the folded alphabook letter sheets on pages 96 to 109 in this book.

Make a cover for the book with a sheet of construction paper folded in half. Print *My Alphabook* on the front. Older children can print the letters by themselves. Provide younger children with alphabet stickers to use on the book cover.

Using Blank Alphabooks

Use one of the following activities to fill the blank Alphabooks:

1. Cut out letters that match, and glue onto the page.

2. Cut out words that start with the letter.

3. Write words that start with the letter.

4. Cut out pictures that start with the letter and glue onto the page.

5. Draw pictures that start with the letter. Place the books in a reading center.

ALPHABOOKS

Making Spiral-Bound Alphabooks

Provide each child with a spiral-bound notebook of any size as long as it has approximately 30 pages.

Use the first inside page as the title page, centering the title on the page. Write each alphabet letter consecutively at the top of each new page. Do not use the backs of pages.

Using Spiral-Bound Alphabooks

Use the Alphabook in one of the following ways:

1. Write a line of uppercase letters.

2. Write a line of lowercase letters.

3. Write a line of upper/lowercase letters.

4. Write words that start with the letter, one word per line.

5. Write words that start with the letter and a short sentence or definition and picture of each word.

Place the books in the reading center.

ALPHABOOKS

Making Magnetic Sheet Photo Album Alphabooks

Make a class book from a magnetic sheet photo album.

Leave the first page for the title and list of authors.

Affix a 2" to 3" (5 to 8 cm) stick-on letter in alphabetical order to the center of each page.

Using Photo Album Alphabooks

Use the magnetic sheet photo album in one of the following ways:

1. Look for small illustrations and photographs of objects that begin with specific letters and glue onto photo-sized pages of paper. Place in photo album.

2. Place photos of other people the class is familiar with on the pages where the letter corresponds to the name. Write each person's name under his or her photo.

3. Draw pictures on photo-sized paper and place in the book.

4. Take photos of objects that start with specific letters and place in the correct order.

5. Collect postcards with objects on them, and let children put them in the right places.

6. Save pictures from old greeting cards. Sort them onto the right pages.

ALPHABOOKS

Making Class Board Alphabooks

Collect 16 sheets of matte board in any size you wish. Bright colors will provide bright backgrounds for collections of pictures.

Put aside three of the sheets to save for the book front, title page and book back.

Put a 2" to 3" (5 to 8 cm) stick-on letter in the upper left-hand corner of each sheet, using both the front and back.

Using Class Board Alphabooks

Use the magnetic sheet photo album in one of the following ways:

1. Assign a page to individual students. Have them collect pictures with their families at home. Bring to school, glue on and label.

2. Assign teams of students to work on individual pages or sets of pages. Collect pictures and label. Observe how students divide up the tasks.

3. Collect labels from boxes, coupons and ads. Glue them onto the correct pages. Make content books by categories—animals, toys, foods.

4. Collect a variety of stickers for children to stick onto the correct pages. Label with the words.

Place the books in centers so children use them. Allow children to read their books to younger classes.

Aa

apple

Ch ch

chair

Alphabooks

Bb

ball

Sh sh

shhhhhh

Cc
cat

Zz
zebra

Dd

dog

Yy

yarn

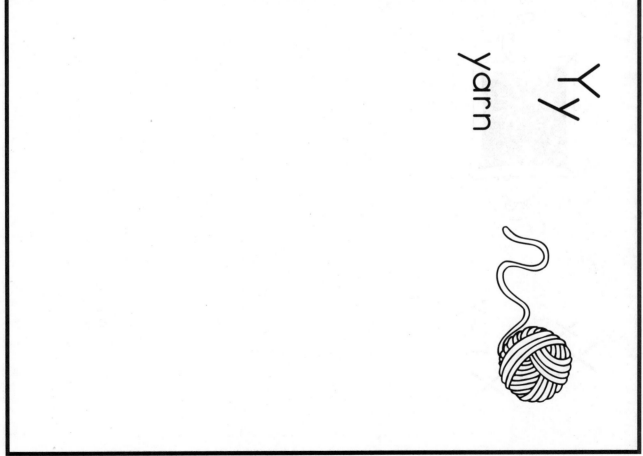

Alphabooks

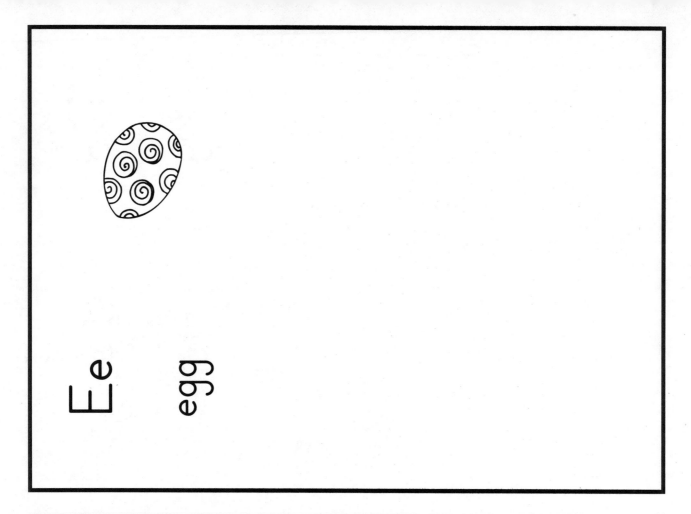

E e

egg

X x

X ray

Ff
fish

Ww
watch

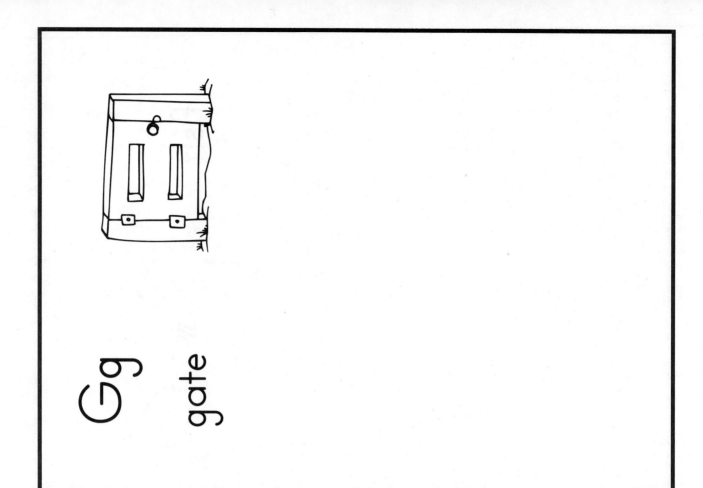

Gg
gate

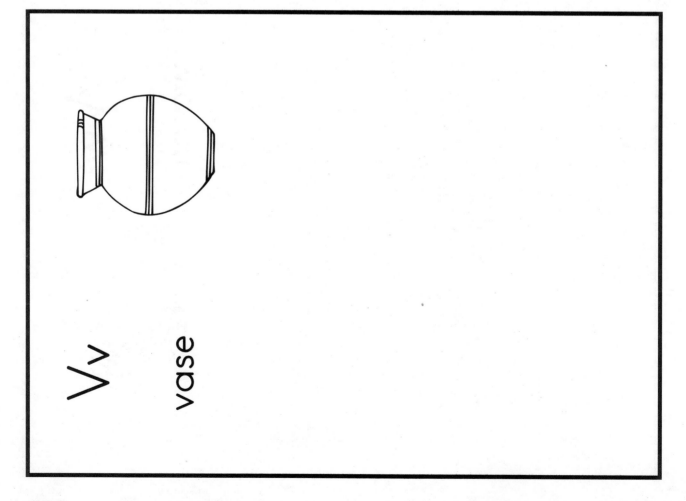

Vv
vase

Hh
hat

Uu
umbrella

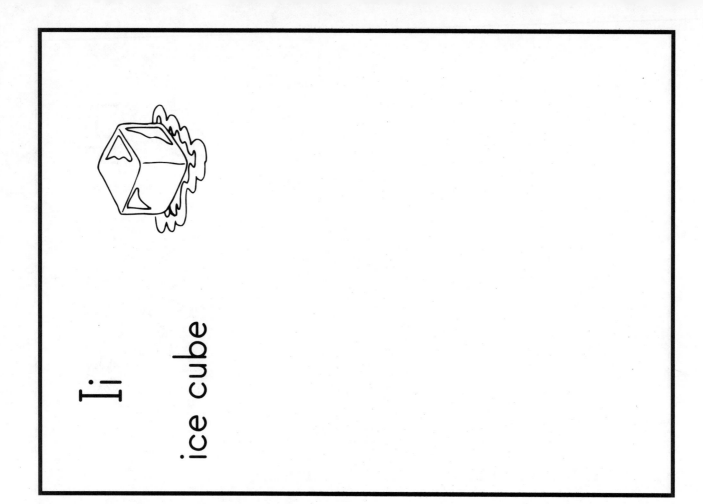

Ii

ice cube

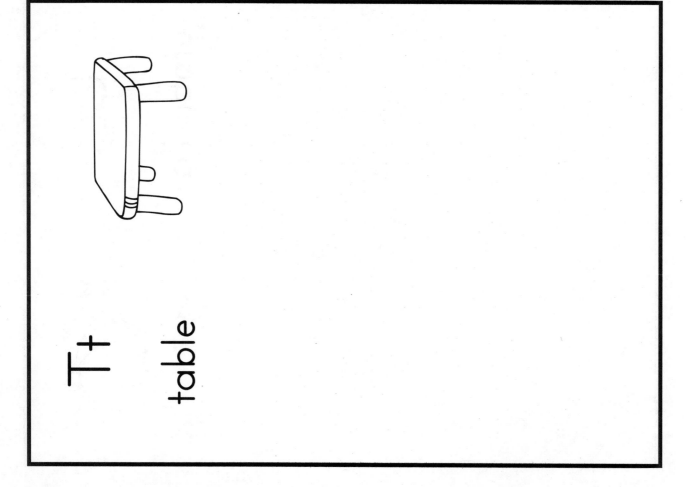

Tt

table

Jj

jelly

Ss

sun

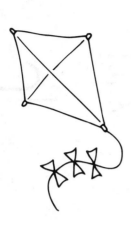

Kk

kite

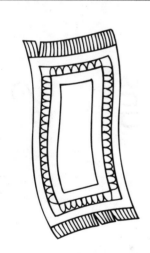

Rr

rug

Ll

lamp

Qq

queen

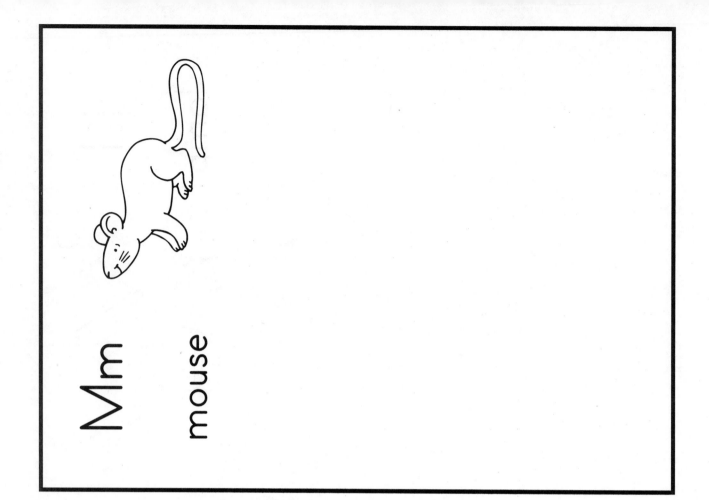

Mm

mouse

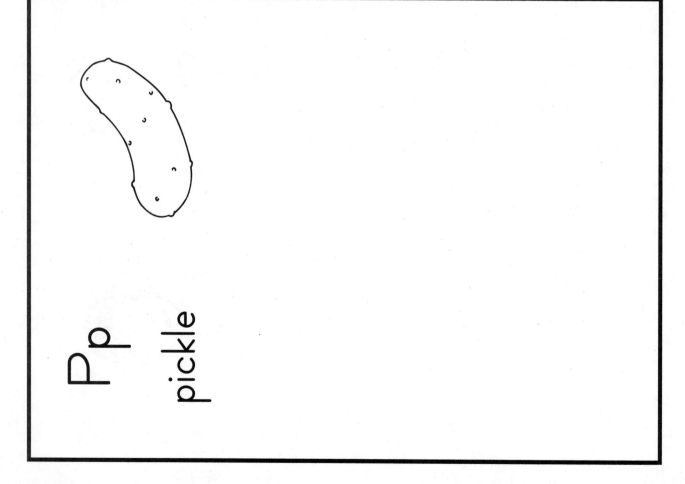

Pp

pickle

Nn

nine

9

Oo

octopus

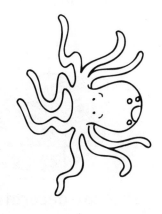

PORTFOLIOS

Containers for Portfolios

stapled contents with cover

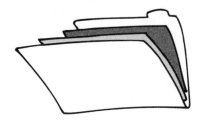

file folders

expanded folders

three-ring folders

student-decorated boxes

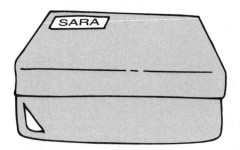

plastic file boxes

PORTFOLIOS

Purposes of Reading Portfolios

Reading portfolios provide evidence of a student's ability in reading, a student's progress in reading and perhaps a student's future goals in reading.

Items to Include in Reading Portfolios

Although you may include all suggested activities, choose some for use in the student's portfolio while permitting the student some choice, too.

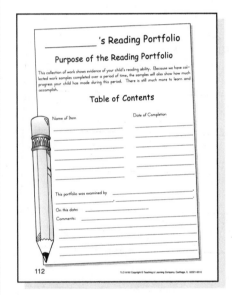

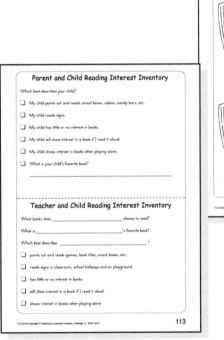

_____ 's Reading Portfolio

Purpose of the Reading Portfolio

This collection of work shows evidence of your child's reading ability. Because we have collected work samples completed over a period of time, the samples will also show how much progress your child has made during this period. There is still much more to learn and accomplish.

Table of Contents

Name of Item   Date of Completion

_____   _____

_____   _____

_____   _____

_____   _____

_____   _____

This portfolio was examined by _____ ,

_____ , _____ .

On this date: _____

Comments: _____

_____

_____

_____

_____

Parent and Child Reading Interest Inventory

Which best describes your child?

☐ My child points out and reads cereal boxes, videos, candy bars, etc.

☐ My child reads signs.

☐ My child has little or no interest in books.

☐ My child will show interest in a book if I read it aloud.

☐ My child shows interest in books when playing alone.

☐ What is your child's favorite book?

_____

- -

Teacher and Child Reading Interest Inventory

What books does _____ choose to read?

What is_____'s favorite book?

Which best describes _____ ?

☐ points out and reads games, book titles, snack boxes, etc.

☐ reads signs in classroom, school hallways and on playground

☐ has little or no interest in books

☐ will show interest in a book if I read it aloud

☐ shows interest in books when playing alone

Inventario de Pariente y Niño Lectura en Interés

¿Cuál describe mejor su niño?

☐ Mi niño apunta y; lee cajas de cereal, videos, dulces, etc.

☐ Mi niño lee senales.

☐ Mi niño tiene poco o ning n interés en libros..

☐ Mi niño toma interés en un libro cuando se lo leo en voz alta..

☐ Mi niño toma interés en libros cuando juega solo.

¿Cuál es el libro favorito de su niño?.

_____

Inventario de Maestro y Niño Lectura en Interés

¿Cuál libro escoge _____ para leer?

¿Cuál es el libro favorito de _____?

¿Cuál mejor describe _____?

☐ apunta y lee juegos, títulos de libros, cajas de bocadillos, etc.

☐ lee las señales en el salón, pasillo o en el campo de recreo.

☐ tiene poco o ningun interés en libros.

☐ toma interés en un libro cuando se lo leo en voz alta.

☐ toma interés en libros cuando juega solo.

My Favorite Stories and Books

Copy the titles from your favorite books in the books below.

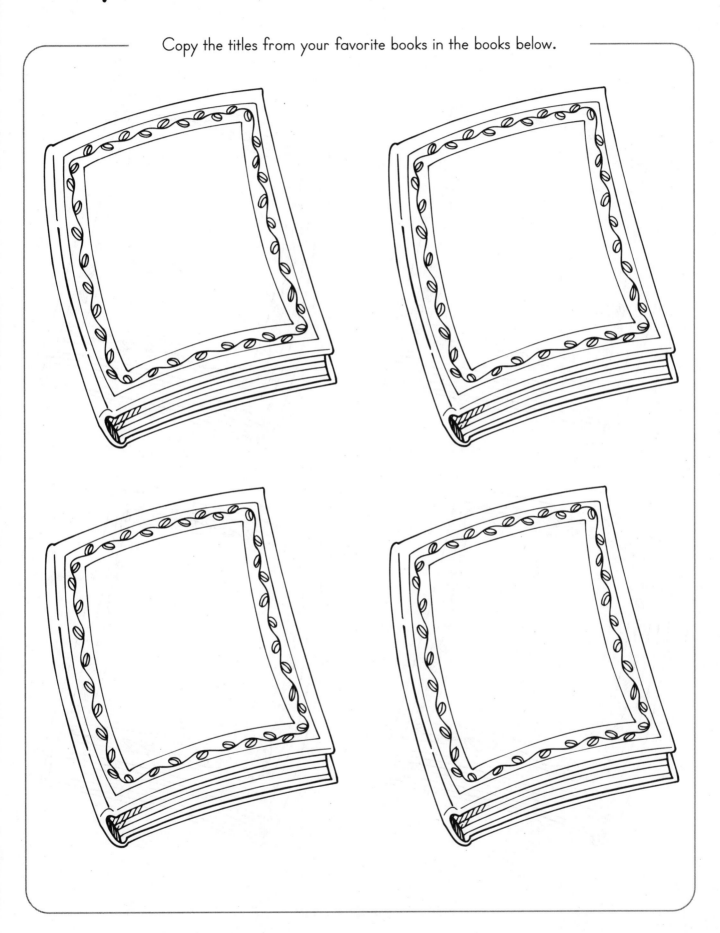

Mis Libros Favoritos

Copea los titulos de tus libros favoritos en los libros abajo.

Home Reading Log

Child's name: _____

Please keep a list of books that you and your child read together or that your child looks at or reads alone.

Book	Date
_____	_____
_____	_____
_____	_____
_____	_____
_____	_____
_____	_____
_____	_____

Which best describes your child when you read a book together?

never	a little	always	
_____	_____	_____	would rather be off playing somewhere
_____	_____	_____	goes to sleep in the middle of the story
_____	_____	_____	listens attentively without interrupting
_____	_____	_____	listens and asks questions throughout the story
_____	_____	_____	reads stories to me using pictures as clues
_____	_____	_____	memorizes stories

Cuenta de Lectura en Casa

Nombre de niño: _____

Por favor haga una lista de libros que usted y su niño lean o que su niño vea o lea solo.

Libro   Fecha

_____   _____

_____   _____

_____   _____

_____   _____

_____   _____

_____   _____

_____   _____

_____   _____

¿Cuál de los siguientes mejor describe a su niño cuando leen juntos?

nunca	un poco	siempre	
_____	_____	_____	quisiera estar jugando
_____	_____	_____	se queda dormido en medio del cuento
_____	_____	_____	escucha atentamente sin interrumpir
_____	_____	_____	escucha y hace preguntas durante el cuento
_____	_____	_____	me lee cuentos usando los dibujos como claves
_____	_____	_____	se memoriza el cuento

School Reading Log

Name: _____

These are books I read at school.

Name of Book	Date	Looks at Pictures	Reads Pictures	Reads Words
_____	_____	_____	_____	_____
_____	_____	_____	_____	_____
_____	_____	_____	_____	_____
_____	_____	_____	_____	_____
_____	_____	_____	_____	_____
_____	_____	_____	_____	_____
_____	_____	_____	_____	_____
_____	_____	_____	_____	_____
_____	_____	_____	_____	_____

Which best describes _____ when reading alone?

never	a little	always	
_____	_____	_____	would rather be playing
_____	_____	_____	sits with and watches while others look at books
_____	_____	_____	looks attentively at a book without interruptions
_____	_____	_____	looks at the pictures and retells the story aloud
_____	_____	_____	reads simple books using word and picture clues
_____	_____	_____	reads simple books using words only

PORTFOLIOS

Purposes of Writing Portfolios

Writing portfolios provide evidence of a student's ability in writing, a student's progress in writing and perhaps a student's future goals in writing.

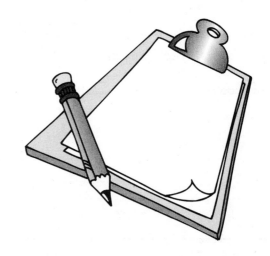

Items to Include in Writing Portfolios

Although you may include all suggested activities, choose some for use in the student's portfolio while permitting the student some choice, too.

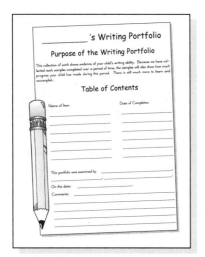

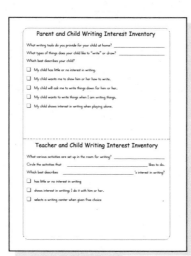

_____ 's Writing Portfolio

Purpose of the Writing Portfolio

This collection of work shows evidence of your child's writing ability. Because we have collected work samples completed over a period of time, the samples will also show how much progress your child has made during this period. There is still much more to learn and accomplish.

Table of Contents

Name of Item   Date of Completion

_____   _____

_____   _____

_____   _____

_____   _____

_____   _____

This portfolio was examined by _____,

_____, _____.

On this date: _____

Comments: _____

_____

_____

_____

Parent and Child Writing Interest Inventory

What writing tools do you provide for your child at home? _____

What types of things does your child like to "write" or draw? _____

Which best describes your child?

☐ My child has little or no interest in writing.

☐ My child wants me to show him or her how to write.

☐ My child will ask me to write things down for him or her.

☐ My child wants to write things when I am writing things.

☐ My child shows interest in writing when playing alone.

- -

Teacher and Child Writing Interest Inventory

What various activities are set up in the room for writing? _____

Circle the activities that _____ likes to do.

Which best describes _____ 's interest in writing?

☐ has little or no interest in writing

☐ shows interest in writing; I do it with him or her.

☐ selects a writing center when given free choice

Inventario de Pariente y Niño Escritura de Interés

¿Qué utensilios de escritura provee usted para su niño en casa? _____

¿Qué tipo de cosas le gusta a su niño "escribir" o dibujar? _____

¿Cuál mejor describe su niño?

☐ Mi niño tiene poco o ningún interés en escribir.

☐ Mi niño quiere que yo le enseñe como escribir.

☐ Mi niño me pide que le escribe las palabras.

☐ Mi niño quiere escribir cuando estoy escribiendo.

☐ Mi niño toma interés en escribir cuando juega solo.

- -

Inventario de Maestro y Niño Escritura de Interés

¿Qué variadades de actividades de escritura hay en el salón? _____

Pon un círculo alrededor de las activades que _____ le gusta hacer.

¿Cuál mejor describe el interés en escritura de _____?

☐ tiene poco o ningún interés en escritura

☐ toma interés en escritura cuando lo hago con el/ella.

☐ selecciona el taller de escritura cuando esta libre para escoger

PORTFOLIOS

── My Favorite Writing ──

Write the name of your favorite activity, sport or experience at the top of one of the notebooks below. Give an example in the space on the notebook.

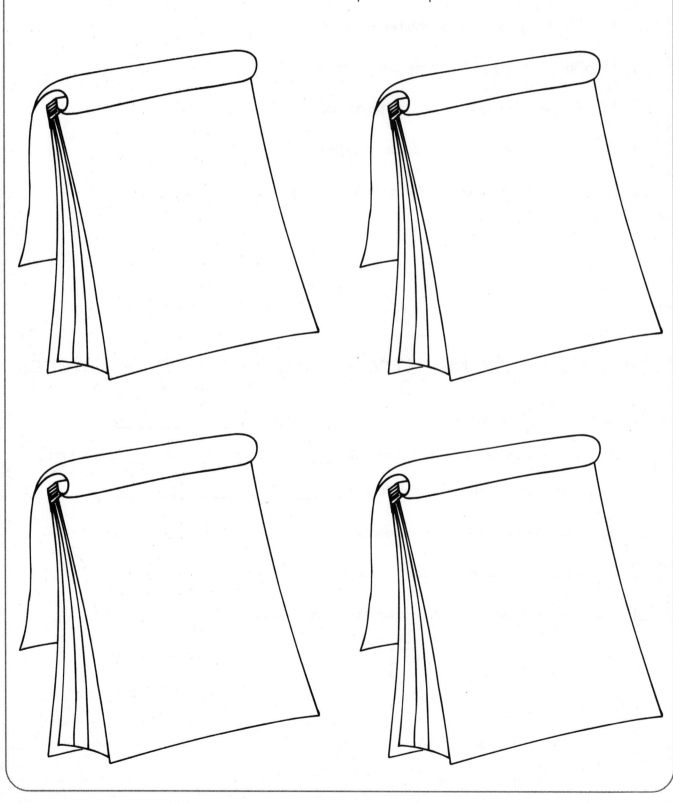

Home Writing Log

Child's name: _____

Please keep writing samples that your child, or you and your child, have completed.

Writing Activity   Date

_____   _____

_____   _____

_____   _____

_____   _____

_____   _____

_____   _____

_____   _____

_____   _____

Which best describes your child when writing?

never   a little   always

_____   _____   _____   would rather be playing

_____   _____   _____   quits in the middle of the activity

_____   _____   _____   works attentively without interruptions

_____   _____   _____   writes and asks questions throughout the session

_____   _____   _____   writes independently and reads it back to me

_____   _____   _____   writes independently and saves items

School Writing Log

Name: _____

These are samples of writing I have done at school.

Name of Writing Activity	Date	Pictures	Labels	Letters	Words	Sentences	Stories
_____	_____	_____	_____	_____	_____	_____	_____
_____	_____	_____	_____	_____	_____	_____	_____
_____	_____	_____	_____	_____	_____	_____	_____
_____	_____	_____	_____	_____	_____	_____	_____
_____	_____	_____	_____	_____	_____	_____	_____
_____	_____	_____	_____	_____	_____	_____	_____
_____	_____	_____	_____	_____	_____	_____	_____
_____	_____	_____	_____	_____	_____	_____	_____
_____	_____	_____	_____	_____	_____	_____	_____
_____	_____	_____	_____	_____	_____	_____	_____

Which best describes _____ when writing alone?

never	a little	always	
_____	_____	_____	would rather be playing
_____	_____	_____	sits with and watches while others write
_____	_____	_____	draws pictures to tell stories
_____	_____	_____	draws pictures with some letter forms
_____	_____	_____	writes some letters to tell stories
_____	_____	_____	phonetically spells words to write stories
_____	_____	_____	writes some sentences to tell stories
_____	_____	_____	writes stories